An Epistle of Comfort

Scriptural Meditations and Passages
for
Persons Suffering from AIDS

by
William Josef Dobbels, SJ

Illustrated and conceived by
William Hart McNichols, SJ

Sheed & Ward

Sheed & Ward™ is a service of National Catholic Reporter Publishing Company, Inc.

Library of Congress Catalog Card Number: 90-60899

ISBN: 1-55612-364-7

Published by: Sheed & Ward
115 E. Armour Blvd. P.O. Box 419492
Kansas City, MO 64141

To order, call: (800) 333-7373

Contents

Dedication

To friends who loved me to life:
Michael & Paul, Linda & Nicki, and Rob
and
To my Jesuit brothers
for taking such wonderful
care of me.

Foreword

Over the past eight years, I have had the privilege of working with and caring for hundreds of persons, both those afflicted with AIDS and their loved ones. While many of these individuals have relinquished their ties with organized religion, the majority are in touch with their own spirituality and cultivate it in their own way. Frequently, these individuals express hurt because of what they perceive to be rejection by Church people because of Church teaching. However, at the same time, there is often a deep hunger and longing for closeness to a Being greater than themselves—be it named God, Higher Power or some other title.

In addition, today, there is great loneliness and sadness among many individuals currently infected with the virus. They have watched friends and associates in their communities deteriorate and die. Often they have been the caregiver for a loved one who, despite all the miracles of modern health care, finally died. A question I hear with increasing frequency is, "Who will be there for me?"

In *An Epistle of Comfort*, Fr. Bill Dobbels relates to many of these questions. From the depths of a rich spirituality and through his personal struggles with the same disease, Fr. Bill is able to speak with tremendous

love and faith and hope of his ever-deepening relationship with his God. His letters to fellow sufferers—his
"dear friends"—are warm invitations to experience and
know God and to grow closer to God because of their
suffering. The style of his letters are affectionate and
profoundly caring.

With wonderful openness and honesty, Fr. Bill identifies with the pain and sadness and loneliness, the fear
and despair, the shame and anger, the darkness and confusion—some or all of which can be an integral part of
the suffering of AIDS. He communicates his knowledge
and understanding of this array of emotions with gentle
sensitivity, but goes beyond these to share his intimate
experiences of an unconditionally loving God. There is
such healing power in his words.

As I read Fr. Bill's letters, I marvel at his simply stated
yet profound insights. I think of how often I would have
welcomed such a book to assist me in comforting my
brothers and sisters who were suffering and grieving so
deeply.

An Epistle of Comfort is a book in which anyone can
find truth and inspiration. It can be opened to any page;
and not only the person with AIDS, but any person who
is suffering—physically, mentally or spiritually—can be
consoled and strengthened by its messages. So, also, can
those who minister to the suffering and bereaved for
they, too, are suffering. Certainly one's powerlessness to
change the course of events, one's own difficulties with
faith and trust in the face of so much sadness and

mystery and one's own secret "why's?" are painful. When we read Fr. Dobbels' opening salutation of each letter, "My dear friend," we know that he wants *all* to be included—the sick and those who love and minister to the sick. He understands because he has been or is where each of his readers is. It is from his condition as "wounded healer" that he ministers to each one of us.

What is most profound for me in these beautiful letters is Fr. Bill's ease in talking about God. In a sense, his words help to alleviate our hunger for God. He invites us to bring our brokenness with great trust to a loving God and to find there a joy and peace and freedom we dared not dream of. Yes, "Even on the road to the cross, we will find that love is stronger than fear, and life—God's life—stronger than death."

Sr. Patrice Murphy, S.C.
St. Vincent's Supportive Care Program
New York, New York

Let nothing perturb you, nothing frighten you.
All things pass;
God does not change.
Patience achieves everything.
Whoever has God lacks nothing
God alone suffices.

—St. Teresa of Avila

Introduction

My dear friend,

That is how I want to address you as you read this book of scriptural meditations for persons with AIDS. I am a shy person, an "introvert" as they say. It takes a lot of courage for me to call you "dear friend"; I do not do it lightly nor out of disrespect.

I call you a dear friend because I love you. I feel intimately connected with you in our mutual suffering of this disease called AIDS. I am writing this just for you. Perhaps after everyone has left your hospital room and the phone is quiet, or maybe when you find yourself alone at home—in one of these moments we can pray and share together the terror, darkness, and, yes, even light and hope of what life has become as a result of having AIDS and all the other various diseases that can accompany the virus.

It has been difficult all my life to let people know that I love them. So what am I doing, a complete stranger to you, telling you that I love you? I know that I do love you and I know a lot of what you have gone through and might go through. My one desire in writing this for you is that somehow and in someway these scriptural readings and meditations can be of comfort for you. In faith and in hope believe that you are not alone.

I am a Catholic priest around 40 years old. I am also a trained Jungian psychotherapist. I love being a priest and I love being a psychologist. I feel at home with men and women of good will no matter what their religious preference is. My good friend, Fr. Bill McNichols, and I have designed this book for anyone suffering from AIDS. You may find that family and friends who do not have AIDS will also benefit from reading this little book. All you need to do is to be open to allowing the Word of God to speak to you and to comfort you.

Three years ago I tested positive for the AIDS virus. These have been some of the worst years of my entire short life. In October of 1987 the doctors diagnosed me with lymphoma and full-blown AIDS. I started an intense regime of chemotherapy at that time to fight the lymphoma. Medical experts thought that—maybe—I might live 5 to 6 months longer from the October diagnosis.

I became very sick as a result of chemotherapy, and long stays in the hospital became routine. Along with the lymphoma I have developed CMV Retinitis, Cryptosporidiosis, Tuberculosis, and Kaposi's Sarcoma. The main point is that I am alive today and I am writing to you. Experts have told me several times that, medically speaking, I should have died by now.

I want to share with you my fears and hopes, the truly graced moments along with the real dark feelings that I have had while fighting this disease. My hope is that you will recognize a part of yourself in this book and thus know in the quiet of your meditation that I love you and that you are not alone. I want to be your companion who is beside you, and being ever-so-quiet and not "in the way" as you and God converse in the silence of your own heart. Over time, and as you grow to trust me as you read these meditations, you will know that I do love you.

How To Use This Book

We want this book of meditations and scriptures to be simple, easy to read and to use. You will notice in the table of contents that there are different chapter headings followed by various scripture readings. It is not necessary for you to read this book in the order of the chapter headings. It will profit you more to go directly to a chapter that best describes how you feel when you sit down to read the book.

Be courageous! If a chapter heading causes either a strong positive or negative reaction from you, chances are that that is the chapter where you will derive the most profit. The Holy Spirit may be drawing you into spiritual consolation or desolation; either way you will benefit greatly by it.

There will be many times that you will not feel any strong spiritual pull one way or the other. That also is good! In either case, try to quiet yourself. Take the phone off the hook and or ask the nurse not to allow anyone to disturb you for 15 to 30 minutes (longer if you need it). Maybe you will get an idea from reading the meditation; something might "click" within you, an idea or a feeling that is trying to come to your consciousness. You might want to keep these ideas written down in your spiritual journal. While reading the scripture, just allow the Word of God to talk to you, to comfort you, to give you an abundance of hope and love. Here it will be you and the Holy Spirit conversing with one another (usually in silence), and this is very holy. Keep in mind what St. Paul wrote in his letter to Timothy (2 Timothy 3:16): "All scripture is inspired by God and is useful for refutation, for correction, and for training in holiness."

Search for someone you can trust with your spiritual journey. As you go through this book it could be very possible that you will gain a lot of insight into your spiritual life. As one learns more about one's spirituality so does one learn more about the very life of God. The two realities go hand in hand.

You may find that you wish to confess past sins or actions that have been bothering you. You may also find that God has whispered something very special to you that you want to share with others. Either way, trust your instincts when choosing someone to talk with you on spiritual matters. There are a lot of very good trained men and women from all religions who are worthy of your trust. But please be careful. There are also ministers, rabbis, nuns and priests who are not ready to hear what you have to say, nor are they able to help you—indeed, they might even do you a lot of harm.

Allow me to give you an example of what happened to me. When I was first diagnosed with lymphoma and AIDS I was in a Catholic hospital. I am fortunate being a priest, because I have dear friends who are either priests or are very spiritual men and women. So when I entered the Catholic hospital I checked on the admissions slip that I did not wish to have a Catholic priest visit me. I did not feel like I wanted to talk with a priest whom I did not know since I already had a priest-friend who knew and loved me. One day as I found myself upset and depressed about being so sick and feeling afraid of what could happen to me, a Catholic chaplain working at the hospital came into my room. I looked up from my bed to see this priest dressed in a surgical gown and wearing latex gloves. He stood about as far from me as he could and as close to the door as he could. I then heard the muffled words of something like, "I'm Father So-and-So, and I wanted to know if you needed to talk to someone . . ."

I felt sick to my stomach. Had I become such a diseased person, so horribly contagious that no one, not even the Church, wanted to touch me? Just what did this priest think he was going to do with me? He could not draw blood from me, so why was he so afraid of me? Was this man, supposedly trained to work with people suffering in a hospital, afraid he might catch a *spiritual* disease from me? How on earth could I relate my deepest felt fears at that moment to anyone so afraid of me? I asked him to leave my room. I then broke down crying.

A spiritual conversation is a special moment filled with tender human contact. A spiritual conversation is not the time to share with those who are so antiseptically guarded that they cannot allow you to touch them emotionally, spiritually or even physically. So be careful. Ask around about whom you might be able to trust with your precious spiritual conversation. Be open to men and women of religions different from your own, who transcend dogma and are in touch with the Spirit of God who loves us all.

My friend, I want to mention two other things that I know are important for you to know and to consider. Too many times I have heard people who do not have AIDS talk about some who have AIDS in this manner: "Well, look at how 'spiritual' people become now that they have come down with AIDS! I happen to know that they never went to church before, yet now all I hear is how 'close to God' they feel. I'm not convinced of their new-found spirituality. I think they are just scared!" In fact, you might now be hesitant to develop a relationship with God because you feel embarrassed for not having had a conscious contact with God for a long time. But, my friend, you must forget these fears and the negative comments that either we or others make.

The first thing I would say to anyone who thinks that those of us with AIDS are "just scared" is, Yes, we are scared!—but not "just" scared. God does not work this way nor does God make us sick in order to make us feel embarrassed. It is true that, whether we are sick or healthy, pride and arrogance will keep anyone from God.

However, God is a God of mercy, *always waiting for us to return* to an active life of prayer, no matter who we are or why we went away from God.

From the beginning of time, holy women and men have reminded us that God is pursuing us and that we can return to God at any moment in our lives. In fact here is what the prophet Isaiah has God saying to us:

"Turn to me and be safe.
all you ends of the earth,
for I am God, there is no
    other!" (Isaiah 45:22)

and

"I have brushed away your offenses
    like a cloud,
your sins like a mist;
return to me,
    for I have redeemed you." (Isaiah 44:22)

The second thing I need to mention to you is the lack of inclusive language in the scriptures. I searched everywhere for a good translation of the Bible that would include language that openly speaks of women and men. I found nothing that was suitable, hence my use of the translation that follows each letter. What I found out is that if you are going to quote a scripture passage you have to quote it exactly as it is printed. I did not have the freedom to change the language to include women in the printed form. Please know that in my letters and in my heart I do include all my sisters for whom I have also written these letters.

Seeking and Longing
for God

As a hart longs for the running waters,
so my soul longs for you, O God.
—Psalm 42

chapter one

Seeking and Longing for God

My dear friend,

Whenever this topic comes up, I take a deep breath. How to write on something so vast and seemingly vague? Yet all the other topics in this meditation book center upon this endeavor: *seeking and longing for God*. After all that I have been through since being diagnosed, the ups and downs, the clarity and the downright darkness that surrounds us, through all this I believe that seeking and longing for God is what motivates us to live. In other words, seeking and longing for God (including the pain that this entails) is why we do the things we do and become the people we become. The search for God directs what we choose to do and choose not to do in life.

The question is, how do I love God who is everywhere? How can I have a personal relationship with Jesus who is "perfect," when it is so clear that I am not? What about all the physical beauty that surrounds us: mountains, lakes, oceans, sunsets, deserts (the list is long)? I believe that God created everything that exists. I cannot create any of these things. How can I feel a personal relationship with someone so powerful?

This disease has taught me firsthand something that I only vaguely understood before. There is the God who created the heavens, the earth and all the beauty therein. I stand in awe before such majesty. What I have learned since being diagnosed with AIDS is to trust and honor the God within me, much more than I did before. When the crowds pressed Jesus for an answer as to when the final time would come about, Jesus told them:

The Kingdom of God is within you! (Lk 17:21) We read in Jn 14:17, "The Spirit of Truth, you know it, because it remains with you, and will be in you."

It's a paradox, a lifelong mystery. God who created us in the very image and likeness of God says in Genesis that all creation is good. There are no exceptions. Creation is so good in the eyes of God that after six days of creating, God declared an international holiday! On the seventh day God rested in order for all to enjoy creation.

We seek God who is totally other and outside of ourselves; yet at the same time we seek and long for the God deep within our hearts. Why do we seek God? Because God first seeks us! As Jesus said, "It was not you who chose me, but I who chose you" (Jn 15:16). God so identifies with us and seeks and longs for us that an inner image of God is part of each of our unique personalities. A true understanding of myself includes the scary recognition that what I seek the most in life, what gives the real meaning to my existence, is God within me. My own inner life—my inner voice, my intuition, my insights, my dreams and my fantasies—are all ways in which God talks to me.

Let me give you a real life example of what I am saying. I can think of no one better who believed that God does indeed speak to us in our imagination than St. Joan of Arc. Joan was born in 1412 in Medieval France to poor peasant farmers. Education was certainly out of the question for Joan, so she too worked the farm in order that her family could survive. One day Joan thought she heard voices within her. In fact the voices could be identified as Michael the Archangel and Saints Margaret and Catherine. France at this time was not only at war with England but was losing the war so badly it looked as if England would claim all of France. The saintly voices told this young, backward, peasant maiden how to beat the English and that she had been chosen to lead the French to victory. Her inner voices further explained that no matter what trials and suffering would be ahead of her, Joan was not to lose faith in God nor in herself. Joan's task was to have a meeting with the King of France and ask him to outfit her with an army.

George Bernard Shaw, in his play "St. Joan," has Joan encounter Captain Robert de Baudercourt, the first official she will need to meet if she is to make it to the King's court. Captain de Baudercourt thinks Joan is crazy and questions her, trying to trip her up. Here is part of the dialogue between the two of them:

Robert: "How do you mean, voices?"

Joan: "I hear voices telling me what to do. They come from God."

Robert: "They come from your imagination."

Joan: "Of course. That's how messages of God come to us!"

I won't go through the entire story, but we know that Joan left her parent's farm and did indeed lead a French army that fought the English. Fighting the English turned out to be the easy part for Joan. At the tender age of nineteen (1431) Joan was accused by the Church of being a heretic and a witch because she maintained that she had heard heavenly voices. How dare this poor peasant proclaim that God would talk to *her*! At Joan's trial theologians tried again and again to trip her up or to get her to recant her position.

In the end Joan stood firm to her faith of having heard the inner voices. The Church burned Joan at the stake declaring she was a heretic and a witch. Joan died a horrible, painful death because she believed in herself. In 1925 this same Church canonized Joan and she became St. Joan of Arc. In doing so the Church proclaimed that Christians could pray to St. Joan and use her life as an example of true courage in keeping the faith in adversity.

Please note that I am not suggesting about people who are suffering severe mental illness and hear voices, that these voices come from heaven and should be followed out. Furthermore we have all had the experience of believing that we were 100% sure inside ourselves what course of action to take or not to take, only to find out later that we were 100% wrong! This is all the more reason why you and I need a good spiritual director and/or therapist who can be objective in helping us to discern the big issues in life.

This may be the biggest challenge of your entire life: to validate your holiness and the holiness of everyone you encounter. Society and our present culture sees very little value in gay people, drug addicts, or anyone who has AIDS. Having AIDS has become for many a moral issue instead of the health issue it truly is. Large groups of Christian men and women condemn people with AIDS, and say AIDS is God's punishment to us and is proof that we are worthless. Countless others "tolerate" us without really knowing who we are. How many people, how many of *us*, truly believe in personal holiness due to the fact that we are all children of God?

Just by being exactly who you are you have the chance to be holy!

Oh, we can run off to our closets and hide our deepest feelings and longing from others and from ourselves— we know how to do that. How many times in the past could you sing a popular country and western song that goes something like, "I was looking for love in all the wrong places!" Lust, greed and prestige seem to offer us a quick fix and relief from our deep longing for love and meaning in our life. The emptiness returns and if we are not careful that emptiness brings with it a cynical, jaded and broken spirit.

Yet the God who created us exactly the way we are loves us and believes in us. And God will not allow us any rest until we believe in the beauty and holiness of life.

Belief in our own inner voice as coming from God has many practical implications for those of us with AIDS. Some contemporary spiritualities encourage us to believe in the divine light and voice within us. I totally agree! With AIDS we enter a medical Twilight Zone like few others do in society. The Medical System finds itself in turmoil as to what to do about AIDS. We have to make decisions about treatment plans, drugs, alternative treatments, no treatments, 1,001 possibilities.

My experience has been to listen carefully to my inner voice which is guiding and leading me to an ability to live with this disease. Knowing when to stop chemotherapy for the lymphoma, or knowing who in my circle of friends and family are truly helpful for me has come from the God who directs my inner life. Trusting my inner life has kept me alive.

Psalm 42:1-6

As the hind longs for the
running waters,
so my soul longs for you, O
God.
Athirst is my soul for God, the
living God.
When shall I go and behold
the face of God?
My tears are my food day and
night,
as they say to me day after
day, "Where is your God?"
Those times I recall,
now that I pour out my soul
within me,
When I went with the throng
and led them in procession to
the house of God,
Amid loud cries of joy and
thanksgiving,
with the multitude keeping
festival.
Why are you so downcast, O
my soul?
Why do you sigh within
me?
Hope in God! For I shall
again be thanking him,
in the presence of my savior
and my God.

Jeremiah 29:12-14

When you call me, when you go to pray to
me, I will listen to you.
When you look for me, you will find me.
Yes, when you seek me with all
your heart, you will find me with
you, says the LORD.

Psalm 63:1-4

O God, you are my God whom
I seek;
for you my flesh pines and my
soul thirsts
like the earth, parched, lifeless
and without water.

Thus I gazed toward you
in the sanctuary
to see your power and your
glory,
For your kindness is a greater
good than life;
my lips shall glorify you.

Psalm 84:2-4

How lovely is your dwelling
place,
O LORD of hosts!
My soul yearns and pines for
the courts of the LORD.
My heart and my flesh
cry out for the living God.
Even the sparrow finds a home,
and the swallow a nest
in which she puts her young—
Your altars, O LORD of hosts,
my king and my God!

Mark 1:35-37

Rising very early before dawn, [Jesus] left and went off to a deserted place, where he prayed.

Simon and those who were with him pursued him and on finding him, said, "Everyone is looking for you."

Matthew 11:28-30

Jesus said: "Come to me, all you who labor and are burdened, and I will give you rest. Take my yoke upon you and learn from me, for I am meek and humble of heart; and you will find rest for yourselves. For my yoke is easy, and my burden light."

Sickness:
Darkness and Loneliness

O Lord, my God, by day I cry out;
at night I clamor in your presence.
—Psalm 88

chapter two

Sickness: Darkness and Loneliness

My dear friend:

The depth of your suffering is known fully only to you and to God. The closest of friends and family who do not have AIDS can only guess at what you are going through. Sickness can be a very lonely business; that's all the more reason you and I need each other.

Sickness changes everything. Rules about how life works and how we form and maintain relationships change as a result of our becoming sick.

Attitudes and opinions undergo a very deep soul-searching, the likes of which I never experienced until I found out that I had AIDS. Like a lot of people who have this disease, I came down with AIDS in the prime of my life. I had just hit my stride in my professional life and felt very good about my personal and spiritual life. I was gearing up to produce and put forth a lot and I knew I could be judged by others by what I did, not necessarily for who I was. Far be it from this culture to find value in the simple fact that "I am." I could and did

15

produce. I could compete and I liked comparing myself to others. Therefore, I was a valuable member of society.

But sickness changes everything. Before becoming sick, I felt that there was a lot of light on my path and I knew just where I wanted to go and how to get there. Now there are days, sometimes weeks and months, where I see nothing but darkness. I can recall many nights in my hospital bed long after friends had left. I would look up and see the IV lines slowly dripping into my veins and I felt such darkness come over my soul. During these times I felt helpless and hopeless. I felt too sick to read or to pray, too anxious to sleep. The moments turned into hours slowly ticking away, giving me no comfort. I did not know for sure if there was a God or only a void. It was of some comfort at times like this to repeat to myself: "This too shall pass." So far it always has. You know what? I feel that after I have gone through these dark experiences, my soul feels stronger. My faith has become more real to me—so real that at times I have felt that I could reach out and touch it.

You may or may not have experienced this darkness of which I speak. If you haven't, it doesn't mean you will or even have to. This darkness is the number one temptation in life that we pray never to have to face; thankfully most people in life do not have to encounter it. Towards the end of the Christian prayer, "Our Father," we say, ". . .and lead us not into temptation, but deliver us from evil." Sickness and fatigue can lead us into the temptation of believing that God does not exist, that life has no meaning and all is dark. The greatest temptation to all mankind is the temptation to despair.

You may find yourself very lonely having this disease. Our culture singles us out, and many of our brothers and sisters with AIDS feel like they are lepers. I hope you don't feel this way because it is not the truth. You may be surrounded by family and friends and still feel loneliness deep inside you.

I know I have. It's like I've crossed a line and I am on the other side of this nightmare. I watch my family and friends who do not have AIDS and they are on the other side. I am facing the possibility of more sickness and death, and they are buying houses or going on trips. All I can worry about is whether I can have enough of an appetite today to eat and not waste away. There are times when I feel so separated and isolated.

There have been days when I wanted to pray but felt so sick from chemotherapy that prayer was impossible. As a rule of thumb I try to keep in mind the following: to the extent that you experience fever, fatigue, low blood counts, diarrhea or even just feeling nauseated, you might be tempted to believe that prayer is useless! When our physical self hurts there is such a temptation to feel hopeless, angry and frustrated. Please my friend, remember it is a temptation! It is not real.

It is very important to remember that on days that you are sick your breathing itself is your prayer. If you can, offer your pain, confusion, fright, and tears to God who sees your suffering and is crying with you. Instead of trying to read this book or even scripture, just recite slowly your favorite prayer and know that you are praying as much as you ever have before.

Maybe you could have someone you love read your favorite passage from scripture or literature (poems, plays, novels, songs) that gives you comfort and touches you. You could quietly look at the pictures in this book or photographs and soak in the silence and make this your prayer. You pray not because you do or produce, but because *You Are*, you exist and are part of this beautiful creation.

Psalm 88

O LORD, my God, by day I cry
out;
at night I clamor in your
presence.
Let my prayer come before
you;
incline your ear to my call for
help.

Psalm 38: 10-13; 22-23

O LORD, all my desire is before
you,
from you my groaning is not
hid.
My heart throbs, my strength
forsakes me,
the very light of my eyes has
failed me.
My friends and my companions
stand back because of my
affliction;
my neighbors stand afar off.
Men lay snares for me seeking
my life;
they look to my misfortune,
they speak of ruin,
treachery they talk of all the
day.

Forsake me not, O LORD;
my God, be not far from me.
Make haste to help me,
O LORD, my salvation.

Matthew 26: 36-40, The Agony in the Garden

Then Jesus came with them to a place called Gethsemane, and he said to his disciples, "Sit here while I go over there and pray." He took along Peter and the two sons of Zebedee, and began to feel sorrow and distress. Then he said to them, "My soul is sorrowful even to death. Remain here and keep watch with me." He advanced a little and fell prostrate in prayer, saying, "My Father, if it is possible, let this cup pass from me; yet, not as I will, but as you will." When he returned to his disciples he found them asleep. He said to Peter, "So you could not keep watch with me for one hour?"

Persecution,
Injustice,
Oppression

Defend the lowly and the fatherless;
render justice to the afflicted
and the destitute.

—Psalm 82

chapter three

Persecution, Injustice, Oppression

My dear friend,

Rare will you be if you have not already experienced some form of injustice because you have AIDS. If you have not experienced either overt or covert oppression, please forgive me if I come across too strongly on this topic. It seems that every time I pick up the newspaper or meet someone with AIDS, I keep hearing or reading story after story of people losing their jobs, housing, or medical benefits. Family members have been known to turn their backs on AIDS patients and walk away in shame about us. Many men, women and children with AIDS feel like social outcasts, all because of public fear and ignorance about AIDS.

If you or I read an account of "big government" stepping on little people we get alarmed and outraged. The type of injustice and oppression I am talking about is more subtle but just as insidious as the stories that make the newspapers.

What I am talking about is the injustice that "good" people are doing to women, men and children with AIDS, out of fear and ignorance. This injustice, as I mentioned, happens at home, in our neighborhoods, at the job place, in the hospital and in churches. You know what I think is the most painful aspect of this injustice? When the people we know and upon whom we depend are the ones who perpetrate the injustice.

Let me give you an example. When I was first diagnosed with AIDS and lymphoma I lived in a small parish house with two other priests in a coastal city. For the entire first year I fought the lymphoma with chemotherapy and made many trips to the hospital and cancer clinic. I was fortunate because I had a loving support group who took care of me. The pastor at that time told me that I was a gift to have around the house.

Towards the end of the year two new young priests moved into the parish house as the former pastor moved out. Behind my back these priests held a meeting and voted to move me out of the house. The reason they wanted me to move was that they felt my being sick would be a burden to them. This was a very painful event for me, and hearing it shocked me as much as first hearing my diagnosis with AIDS. Here were fellow priests meeting behind my back and not allowing me to give any input into their trying to understand my situation. The move from this parish house would also necessitate my having to leave the city that I loved and in which I felt at home. Just like that, they asked me to leave my peers, support group, and all the medical personnel with whom I had been working!

The priest who organized this move to kick me out of the house told me that he thought I was living a "cushy" life with few responsibilities. I had taken a medical leave of absence from school and was not saying Mass at the parish. In total desperation I moved back to the Midwest because at that time there were no other options for me. With the tremendous sense of loss and feelings of rejection, I honestly thought I was going to die soon. I was starting to buckle under the added stress this caused me; losing my home and loving friends, I no longer knew why I was fighting to stay alive.

I want to be clear about something. This was not the Catholic Church kicking me out of my home, it was three or four men doing it in an isolated event. Fellow priests in the Midwest heard what was going on and made it clear to me that they would welcome me with open arms and take care of me if needed. This is my point: don't be shocked when you hear about or experience injustice from people you know and whom you expect to be able to trust in your vulnerable state.

The Injustice of Innocent Suffering

My friend, I want to touch upon an area where you and I are the most fragile, bruised and confused: the injustice of innocent suffering and our relationship with God. How many times have I felt anger (if not rage) with God for allowing me and my friends to suffer so much and in so many ways? If this is not a punishment then why doesn't God do something to stop my suffering? I know these feelings affect everyone in some form or another. I read about natural disasters, planes being shot down from the sky with many innocent lives lost. At times I shake my fist at God! Our faith in Life and in God is sorely being tested.

Some say to me, "The Lord has cut you down." I don't understand what this means. What on earth did I do to "deserve" this physical and emotional suffering with its attendant feelings of panic and fear? It just does not make sense to me and this may not make any sense to you.

There are others (usually people without this disease) who say they know and that they understand "why" these things happen; but my friend, I must confess, I do not. True, in the past I was not a "saint," but neither was I such a hardened psychopathic criminal as to deserve this. The only people who make sense to me are my friends like you. You, my friend, who are suffering and "know" what suffering is all about, you are the one to whom I listen and from whom I get my comfort.

There are a few people who do not have this disease who are spiritually wise and are out in the forefront helping us. These people and the ones I know who are suffering say the same thing when it comes to the question of "why is there innocent suffering?"

"*We don't know why!*" It's the only statement I now trust. I find it excruciatingly painful when some people tell me that I unconsciously brought all this suffering on myself in order to "learn" something. This somewhat facile explanation of a deep mystery just doesn't fit for me; it makes me feel even more guilty when I don't get better.

It is as if we have run head-on into a big brick wall and it stops us in our tracks. The big brick wall is that, when push comes to shove, we do not and cannot know the full nature and mind of God. God who is totally "Other" is revealed to us and yet remains elusive. Our souls stand naked before the presence of God. We live with the knowledge that we trust ourselves and the meaning of Life itself to a completely "Other" being or "higher power." God is outside ourselves and we can never know God as fully as we are known by God. The image of God to whom we pray and to whom we relate is highly subjective and different for each of us. It would seem that God would not have it any other way, as long as we remain aware that God is radically and totally "Other."

In the prophet Isaiah (46:5, 9-10) we read:

"Whom would you compare me
    with, as an equal.
or match me against, as
    though we were alike?

"I am God, there is no other,
    I am God, there is none like
      me.
At the beginning I foretell the

outcome;
in advance, things not yet
done.
I say that my plan shall stand,
I accomplish my every purpose."

We cannot box in God with our desires to define God once and for all, and therefore think that we know God and all God's plans. God does not bend nor give in to our obsession to control.

God created everything and God is in control, not us. I don't mean this to be a tug-of-war between ourselves and God as to who is in charge. I just think it is part of spiritual maturity to accept and to live with the reality that in innocent suffering we come face to face with a reality that we do not understand. We cannot fully comprehend what God is doing or not doing. This is a mystery before which I can only stand in silence; my heart bursting with questions, darkness and pain.

My friend, exactly at this point the ultimate temptation lures us: "Since I cannot and do not understand innocent suffering, I cannot believe in God, let alone a so-called loving God." This temptation soon leads to despair.

Isaiah 53:7-9

Though he was harshly treated,
he submitted
and opened not his mouth;
Like a lamb led to the slaughter
or a sheep before the shearers,
he was silent and opened not
his mouth.
Oppressed and condemned, he
was taken away,
and who would have thought
any more of his destiny?
When he was cut off from the
land of the living,
and smitten for the sin of his
people,
A grave was assigned him
among the wicked
and a burial place with
evildoers.
Though he had done no wrong
nor spoken any falsehood.

Matthew 10: 26-31
Courage under Persecution

Jesus said: "Therefore do not be afraid of them. Nothing is concealed that will not be revealed, nor secret that will not be known. What I say to you in the darkness, speak in the light; what you hear whispered, proclaim on the housetops. And do not be afraid of those who kill the body but cannot kill the soul; rather, be afraid of the one who can destroy both soul and body in Gehenna.

"Are not two sparrows sold for a small coin? Yet not one of them falls to the ground without your Father's knowledge. Even all the hairs of your head are counted. So do not be afraid; you are worth more than many sparrows."

The Prayer for Peace
St. Francis of Assisi

Lord, make me an instrument of your
    peace.
Where there is hatred, let me sow love;
    where there is injury, pardon.
    where there is doubt, faith;
    where there is despair, hope;
    where there is darkness, light;
    where there is sadness, joy.
O Divine Master, grant that I may not so
    much seek
    to be consoled, as to console;
    to be understood, as to understand;
    to be loved, as to love.
For it is in giving that we receive;
    it is in pardoning that we are pardoned;
    and it is in dying that we are born to
        eternal life.

Sin
and
Suffering

Cleanse me of sin with hyssop,
that I may be purified;
Wash me, and I shall be whiter
than snow.

—Psalm 51

chapter four

Sin and Suffering

My dear friend,

As we talk about sin and suffering, the very first thing I want to talk with you about is the Number One initial feeling most people have upon receiving a diagnosis of AIDS: *Guilt.*

This guilt arises because we think that somehow and in some way we have sinned or have done something terribly wrong, and AIDS is the punishment for having done this wrong. We do not know exactly what it is we have done wrong but we know we feel bad about ourselves. We feel diseased and ugly. Isn't that proof enough that we have sinned?

Unfortunately, very early in the AIDS epidemic, conservative fundamentalists (usually calling themselves Christian) publicly declared that AIDS was a punishment from God. These people argued that AIDS is a proof that God wants to rid society of certain drug addicts or sexual deviates.

Please, my friend, don't believe this junk spirituality for one minute! My friend, please be careful because this demeaning attitude about sinning and getting AIDS is even present in men and women who do not consider themselves fundamentalist Christians. Who for a second wants to believe in the unmerciful and punishing god of these fundamentalists?

As in all things neither I nor anyone else can "prove" to you what we accept in faith as the true nature of God. Trust your heart in this and all matters. If you had a child, as some of us with AIDS do, would you ever in your right mind inflict the suffering of AIDS on this child you love—just to punish him or her? The cruelty of this punishment would never, could never, be commensurate with any "crime" your child may have committed. If you and I would never inflict AIDS on a child, how on earth can we fall for the notion that a forgiving and loving God would do this? If this whole notion of getting AIDS as a means of God's punishment does not make sense to you—good. It shouldn't.

Suffering, innocent or not, is a deep mystery. The notion that God inflicts the suffering of AIDS is too easy a way out of a complicated and intricate problem. It makes the relationship between God and ourselves so black and white; you and I know it just isn't that simple.

This disease catches us all at various stages along life's path. We need to be honest with ourselves now more than ever before. This means that before AIDS, we were, to some degree, alienating others and isolating ourselves from life. To the extent that we isolated and alienated ourselves before being diagnosed, the chances are that we still have a lot of work to do on ourselves. AIDS or no AIDS, many of us still need to grow up.

Upon the first diagnosis of AIDS, these problem areas got swept away because of the intensity of the medical news we received. I know for myself that with chemotherapy fighting the lymphoma it took almost a full year before I realized that I still had some relationships that needed healing. I and the ones involved left our relationships "on hold" from the time I was first diagnosed. But the problems did not go away, they were waiting for us. Having AIDS has not removed any of my personal problems nor does AIDS exempt me from doing my part to help heal life's hurts.

Since I am a priest, several of my friends, Christian and non-Christian, believers and nonbelievers, have asked me "what is a sin?" The best reply I can give, the one that makes most sense to me, is that sin is the denial of life. I am not talking about suicide here, nor do I pass any judgment on suicide. Most sin is subtle and escapes our consciousness. Let me try to explain. Life says "YES" and sin says "NO." Sin is the large and small ways we try to take life away from ourselves and from others. Sin is denying others the right to be exactly who they are right now and trying to make them over in an image that suits *us* best. Sin denies life as it is right now. Sin is the attempts we make in trying to fashion the world around us according to our individual and selfish needs. Sin is the subtle way we try to play God.

Sin is always some form of a lie. Lying is unreal (denies life) whereas truth (rigorous, honest truth) is real. "Lying" includes a refusal to look at our own dark sides; a subtle belief that it does not matter if we look at ourselves honestly or not; Lying means telling ourselves that only "big" sins (murder, thief, etc.) have any effect upon us, so why bother with the rest?

Sin is present when we refuse to take care of ourselves or others when opportunities are presented. There is sin in psychological abuse of others as well as in our neurotic obsessions over past hurts. We can get so caught up about past hurts (real or imagined) that we deny life by missing what we are doing in the present.

We are still fully human and fully alive and we are responsible for our behavior. I rejoice in this because contrary to our feelings, we remain part of the human family. AIDS cannot remove our human capacity to sin. Yes, there are days when I am more cranky and have a lower level of tolerance because of this illness. I believe that I am still responsible for how I treat others.

I don't know about you but I notice that since having AIDS I have become more introspective and self-centered. A lot of this is good and important and has helped me to take excellent care of myself. But it can also become so self-centered that I don't notice others who come in and out of my daily life and who are them-selves in pain. It helps to take notice of nurses, doctors, support-service people, as well as family and friends who need us to touch them and let them know how important they are to us. Ask someone how *they* are today and be open and present to them as someone who cares.

Psalm 51: 9-19
The Miserere: Prayer of Repentance

Cleanse me of sin with hyssop,
that I may be purified;
wash me, and I shall be whiter
than snow.
Let me hear the sounds of joy
and gladness;
the bones you have crushed
shall rejoice.
Turn away your face from my
sins.
and blot out all my guilt.

A clean heart create for me, O
God,
and a steadfast spirit renew
within me.
Cast me not out from your
presence,
and your holy spirit take not
from me.
Give me back the joy of your
salvation,
and a willing spirit sustain in
me.

O LORD, open my lips,
and my mouth shall proclaim
your praise.
For you are not pleased with
sacrifices;
should I offer a holocaust, you
would not accept it.

My sacrifice, O God, is a
contrite spirit;
a heart contrite and humbled,
O God, you will not
spurn.

Matthew 7:1-5,
Judging Others

Jesus told us, "Stop judging, that you may not be judged. For as you judge, so will you be judged, and the measure with which you measure will be measured out to you. Why do you notice the splinter in your brother's eye, but do not perceive the wooden beam in your own eye? How can you say to your brother, 'Let me remove that splinter from your eye,' while the wooden beam is in your eye? You hypocrite, remove the wooden beam from your eye first; then you will see clearly to remove the splinter from your brother's eye."

1 John 1:5-10, God is Light

Now this is the message that we have heard from
him and proclaim to you:
God is light,
and in him there is no darkness at all.
If we say,
"We have fellowship with him,"
while we continue to walk in darkness,
we lie and do not act in truth.
But if we walk in the light
as he is in the light,
then we have fellowship
with one another,
and the blood of his Son Jesus
cleanses us from all sin.
If we say,
"We are without sin,"
we deceive ourselves,
and the truth is not in us.
If we acknowledge our sins,
he is faithful and just and
will forgive our sins
and cleanse us from every wrongdoing.
If we say,
"We have not sinned,"
we make him a liar,
and his word is not in us.

Forgiveness

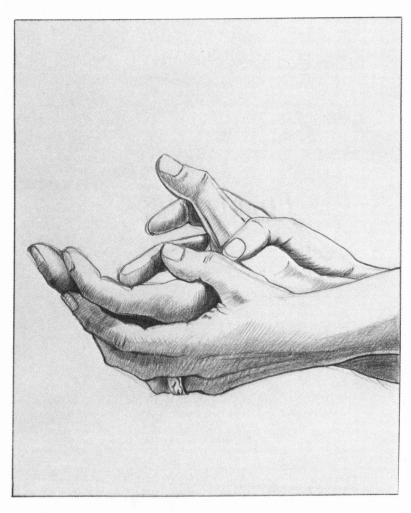

But with you is forgiveness.
—Psalm 130

chapter five

Forgiveness

My dear friend,

The only reason we talked at all about "sin" in the above letter is because of the reality of forgiveness. Without the possibility of forgiveness there is no reason to examine sin and its consequences. However, as I sit down to write to you and share some ideas on the importance and nature of forgiveness, I feel that I will choke on my words.

Some days forgiveness of myself and of others seems like the last thing in the world I want to do or can do. I have been thinking about what I told you in Chapter Three on "Injustice," and how others forced me to move from the place I considered my home. With vivid memories of such an ugly and painful event, I am trying to find some value and meaning in forgiveness. Make no mistake about it, forgiveness takes a lot of courage, patience, and faith; trust me, I know!

So why do I even bother you about it? I still believe, in the midst of this confusion called "AIDS," that learning how to forgive and doing it is one of the best things you and I can do to take care of ourselves. In our weakened physical state it may be one of the few things we can still do. I don't know why, but whenever there is real forgiveness (*for* others or *from* others) there issues forth a real sense of peace and calm. When broken hearts cry out to be mended, the best medication does not come from an IV drip bag but rather from forgiveness.

Like many of us, you might be aware of any number of "12-Step" programs that are helping people overcome addictions. People addicted to alcohol, drugs, food, sex (you name it) are finding a way out of their personal hell by practicing a simple and difficult reality: forgiveness. It takes a lot of work and effort to live a life of forgiveness. But forgiveness can and does happen, and people are becoming more alive and peaceful as a result of doing it.

I spent way too many years not wanting to forgive people in my life or certain painful events of my past. I clobbered them, and others, with feelings of resentment, waiting for them to "make it up to me." What I found out was that the only person I was clobbering was myself. I do not know why it happens, but whenever I hold a grudge or won't forget a past hurt, I am the one who keeps hurting—no one else. For me the route to much more peace, happiness and self-esteem has been along the path of forgiveness.

Today some people proclaim that learning how to forgive ourselves and others is the most important task we have before us. I totally agree with them, especially Louise Hay. Louise Hay's meditation tapes on forgiveness and letting go of past hurts has been a great treasure for myself and many others. Keep in mind that there is nothing "new" about the value and need for forgiveness. All major religions preach forgiveness as the hallmark of their message. One gets the impression (correctly) that forgiveness is very important to God. The number one reason Jesus came to earth was to lead a life of forgiveness and thus show by his example the value and need for us to do likewise. And yet, my friend, how much of this forgiveness have your heard, even from the pulpits? We *all* seem to struggle putting forgiveness into practice.

You and I have a chance to change that for the better. If anyone in the world is watching us, we have something to teach the world. I know that when we are very sick it feels like we are very powerless, mere cogs on a wheel. But, in faith, we have a lot of power because we can still, if we choose, learn over and over again how to forgive. AIDS may take my physical body from me but it cannot take my soul. From those of us to whom much injustice and oppression has happened emerge powerful men and women who practice the art of forgiveness. Here again I don't want to come off sounding like I am proposing that the road to spiritual happiness is easy. Again, forgiveness takes courage, patience, and a lot of faith. I know first-hand that sometimes it is painful to forgive.

Upon hearing of my diagnosis of AIDS and lymphoma the first person I needed to forgive was myself. I felt so "down on myself" and so very stupid. Immediately I assumed that catching AIDS was a sure sign of how much I hated myself and how, unconsciously, I wanted to die. I felt not only physically sick, but emotionally beaten up. There are some current philosophies and spiritualities that even promote this attitude and maintain that the purpose of AIDS is to teach a lesson. Honestly, I do not know where these people get their revelations and I don't mean to debate the pros and cons here in my letter today. All I know is that I gained much more peace and calm in my heart when I did forgive myself for getting AIDS. Forgiveness of self and of others brings about a huge reduction of stress—and you know the value of that by now!

Let's not shy away from the next most difficult person we need to forgive for this mess. God. Many different arguments run through my head. "How dare I say I need to forgive God who is all knowing and all powerful, just who do I think I am?" "Forgive God *for what?*—since I don't believe that God gave me AIDS to punish me in the first place." My friend, it all sounds very confusing. My gut intuition is that somehow and someway if we are ever to believe that we love God, we have to forgive God. Forgiving God would entail first getting in touch with the anger and rage we have with God for letting us get this disease in the first place. Maybe, just maybe, forgiving God is a step toward understanding innocent suffering.

My friend, I wanted to mention an important, albeit touchy, aspect of "turning the other cheek" and forgiving others. You may be called upon to forgive someone in your life who has caused you a lot of pain. You may find that you need to forgive a parent, brother or sister, friend or lover who has physically and/or emotionally abused you. What I am talking about here is real hurt. But after you have forgiven someone who abused you, please don't get back in line for more abuse.

If a family member, or anyone, for that matter, has refused to love you for who you are, please do not allow them to continue to stress you out and make you angry. Forgiving someone and "turning the other cheek" does not mean you cannot and should not remove this person from your inner circle of family and friends. You may find, as I have, close friends or family members who take your disease much too personally and are unable to support you. These people get hysterical and frightened about what your being sick means to them. Many people still harbor unfounded fears that somehow and in some way they are going to catch some disease from you. You will hear subtle remarks about what your being sick is doing to them. What these remarks do is increase your feelings of guilt. You may need to remove these people from being around you and even talking with you on the phone. You don't need these people at this time in your life and you have to protect yourself from the stress that they generate. The best thing you can give any family member or friend is to be a person who is taking excellent care of herself or himself.

Psalm 86:1-7, 12
Prayer in Time of Distress

Incline your ear, O LORD;
answer me,
for I am afflicted and poor.
Keep my life, for I am devoted
to you;
save your servant who trusts
in you.
You are my God; have pity on
me, O LORD,
for to you I call all the day.
Gladden the soul of your servant,
for to you, O LORD, I lift up
my soul;
For you, O LORD, are good and
forgiving.
abounding in kindness to all
who call upon you.
Hearken, O LORD, to my prayer
and attend to the sound of my
pleading.
In the day of my distress I call
upon you,
for you will answer me.

I will give thanks to you, O
LORD my God,
with all my heart,
and I will glorify your name
forever.

Psalm 103:1-5
Praise of Divine Goodness

Bless the LORD, O my soul;
and all my being, bless his
holy name.
Bless the LORD, O my soul,
and forget not all his benefits;
He pardons all your iniquities,
he heals all your ills.
He redeems your life from
destruction,
he crowns you with kindness
and compassion,
He fills your lifetime with
good;
your youth is renewed like the
eagle's.

Psalm 130
Prayer for Pardon and Mercy

Out of the depths I cry to you,
O LORD;
Lord, hear my voice!
Let your ears be attentive
to my voice in supplication:

If you, O LORD, mark iniquities,
Lord, who can stand?
But with you is forgiveness,
that you may be revered.

I trust in the LORD;
my soul trusts in his word.
My soul waits for the LORD
more than sentinels wait for
the dawn.

More than sentinels wait for
the dawn,
let Israel wait for the LORD,
For with the LORD is kindness
and with him is plenteous
redemption;
And he will redeem, Israel
from all their iniquities.

Luke 5:17-26
The Healing of a Paralytic

One day as Jesus was teaching, Pharisees and teachers of the law were sitting there who had come from every village of Galilee and Judea and Jerusalem, and the power of the Lord was with him for healing.

And some men brought on a stretcher a man who was paralyzed; they were trying to bring him in and set [him] in his presence. But not finding a way to bring him in because of the crowd, they went up on the roof and lowered him on the stretcher through the tiles into the middle in front of Jesus. When he saw their faith, he said, "As for you, your sins are forgiven."

Then the scribes and Pharisees began to ask themselves, "Who is this who speaks blasphemies? Who but God alone can forgive sins?" Jesus knew their thoughts and said to them in reply, "What are you thinking in your hearts? Which is easier, to say, 'Your sins are forgiven,' or to say, 'Rise and walk'? But that you may know that the Son of Man has authority on earth to forgive sins"—he said to the man who was paralyzed, "I say to you, rise, pick up your stretcher, and go home." He stood up immediately before them, picked up what he had been lying on, and went home, glorifying God.

Then astonishment seized them all and they glorified God, and, struck with awe, they said, "We have seen incredible things today."

Love

*The favors of the Lord I will
sing forever.*
—Psalm 89

chapter six

Love

My dear friend,

First let me share with you a quote from Oscar Wilde that I think you will like:

"Where there is no extravagance there is no love,
Where there is no love there is no understanding."

I quote Oscar Wilde because I know that great poets and writers throughout history have written much more eloquently on love than I ever could. This morning, as I was giving myself an IV medication to fight blindness (CMV Retinitis), I found myself fretting. How would I define or even talk with you about "love"? Not only have countless others attempted definitions of love but we know that songs and stories about love lost, love found or love desired fill the airwaves.

I remember a story about a newsman who asked a Supreme Court Justice if he could define pornography. The Justice replied, "No I cannot define pornography, but I know it when I see it." That's exactly how I feel about writing you today on such an important, yet elusive topic called "Love." My friend, I cannot define love but I know it when I see it. I think that love is something you have to experience or it means nothing. Let me explain.

Since being diagnosed with AIDS I have experienced countless times of real healing love from others. One of the main reasons that I am alive today and able to write to you is because people love me and I know it. Love has kept me alive by giving me a reason to keep fighting and wanting to live. When I say that I have experienced love I am talking about love as a two-way street. In other words, others have loved and touched me and have allowed me to love and to touch them.

Yes, there is the type of love given to us by caretakers who provide much-needed services for us. We take in their love and care and our souls are refreshed. Without these women and men who are fighting for our rights and our lives we would be lost. The type of love that has saved my life and has made my life a beautiful place in the midst of suffering is when someone has loved me enough to grow and change through this disease with me.

Let me give you an excellent example of real love. I mentioned to you that others forced me to move from a home that was a tremendous support and comfort to me. The people bringing about this momentous change in my life did not want me to be a "burden" on them. Tearfully I called a close friend of mine and related the events as they had happened and what all was going on.

I had accepted the opinion of me that the people asking me to move were putting forth: *I Am A Burden*! I felt ugly, useless, and, like disposable trash, I should have been thrown away.

My friend's love instantly changed all that. Without a second's hesitation my friend said, "Of course you are a burden. It's a burden to see you suffer and hurt and not be able to do anything about it. It's a burden to know that you could die from this and I will lose you. Of course you are a burden, how on earth can someone have AIDS and NOT be a burden?" Then my friend went on to say, "But what a precious burden you are! What in life is worth living for if not to help carry the burdens of those you love. How can anyone escape the "burdens" that are all around us?" My friend, I got his point immediately. While I cannot define love to you, I know that in that moment real love was staring me in the eyes.

My friend, when I say that I love you, I love you for who you have been in the past and who you have become and will become as a result of AIDS.

Family, Friends and Love: Three Groups

I offer the following remarks neither to condemn nor to make anyone feel guilty. You and I are very vulnerable and more than ever before we need to protect ourselves. Keep in mind that the following remarks do not include everyone who comes in and out of our lives. I offer these remarks to you with the hope that they will bring understanding to some of the feelings you may have.

When it comes to family and friends who knew me before I got AIDS, I have found that I could place them in one of three groups. The First Group consists of people who became hysterical when they found out my diagnosis. At first these people flattered me with much intense, emotional outpouring. But with time I found that these friends or family members were using my illness to focus their attention on anything but their own growth issues. In other words, as long as they could be so worried about me and worried about AIDS, these people did not have to concentrate on things that needed changing in their own lives. Since they had me to worry about how could they worry about themselves?

This first group's intense concern turned out to be self-centered. I know that this may sound strange to you, but I felt *used* by these people. I started hearing things like, "You have no idea how hard it has been on me knowing you are sick." "It hurts me so much to see you suffering like this." I got the impression that they worried more about their own pain than what I might be going through. My friend, some people call this type of attention "love," but I cannot.

The Second Group of family and friends are different from the first group. Before my diagnosis with AIDS, people in this group and I felt very close to each other. With members of this group I spent many hours of happiness, fun, and long talks where we shared our souls.

As a caretaker (priest and psychologist) these people told me that I had been a great influence in their lives. I feel that we truly loved and cared for each other. Then something drastic happened and I became very sick. As a result of AIDS I had to let go of caretaking for anyone but myself.

In the beginning, people in this second group stayed by my side with letters, cards, phone calls or visits. I could see the pain and disbelief on their faces as they tried to be with me. As you and I know, AIDS develops slowly. Most of us have been sick now for a long time. It was subtle at first but I started noticing that some of my friends and family had stopped calling or seeing me. I even would write a few of them and get no response. I felt rejected and the silence was painful. Sometimes five to six months would pass before I would hear from one of these friends. When I did finally hear from them the whole tone was as if nothing had happened and no time had passed since we last talked.

I have given this second group a lot of thought. My friend, I do not want to come off sounding like I am accusing anyone of anything. I am just trying to make some sense out of this confusion. Here is a group of people from whom and to whom I felt a lot of love. Now, over time with this disease, I feel quite distant from these people. How did it happen? The feeling I get from people like this is that they loved me but did not want me to change. As long as I was happy and "up," I was great to know and to be around. The feeling I get from them is, "How dare you get sick. You got

AIDS, not us, and we are not going to let AIDS change our lives!" Staying away from me allows them not to have to think about suffering and their own death. I think there are some people who just cannot stand the pain involved in loving you when you are so sick. What I am about to say is as hard to swallow as some of the medication we have to take to fight AIDS.

The type of "love" from this second group is not what you need at this stage of your life. This type of "on again-off again" love stresses us out. Lovingly and with no small pain, you may need to let these people go and to love them from afar.

Those of us with AIDS suffer the physical, emotional and spiritual effects of this disease. Remember, if someone is going to love us as we are now (and not as we were in the past), that person is going to suffer from AIDS also. There is no way out and that is the reason a lot of people run from us. We have the physical AIDS, but the ones who stay next to us have a spiritual and emotional AIDS. These people are in what I call the Third Group and it is their extravagant love that keeps us alive. This is an example of extravagant, understanding and real love: the willingness to suffer and to change for a loved one suffering with AIDS.

The people in this third group are the ones who allow themselves to feel helpless as they see us suffer and they do not run away. Not only do these people face their own death, they do not hide from their anger or rage against God, the seemingly slow-moving Medical Community or Federal Government. Staying close to us changes their whole world and they meet the challenge with tenderness, compassion, tears and confusion. Small wonder that we with AIDS feel so close to them.

To stand next to us through this ordeal is a momentous task and few can meet the challenge. You want to know what God looks like? Look into the face of someone who loves you this way!

Mark 12:28-31
The Greatest Commandment

One of the scribes, when he came forward and heard them disputing and saw how well he had answered them, asked him,

"Which is the first of all the commandments?"

Jesus replied, "The first is this: 'Hear, O Israel! The Lord our God is Lord alone! You shall love the Lord your God with all your heart, with all your soul, with all your mind, and with all your strength.'

"The second is this: 'You shall love your neighbor as yourself.' There is no other commandment greater than these."

1 Corinthians 13: 1-7, 12-13
The Way of Love

If I speak in human and angelic tongues but do not have love, I am a resounding gong or a clashing cymbal. And if I have the gift of prophecy and comprehend all mysteries and all knowledge; if I have all faith so as to move mountains but do not have love, I am nothing. If I give away everything I own, and if I hand my body over so that I may boast but do not have love, I gain nothing. Love is patient, love is kind. It is not jealous, love is not pompous, it is not inflated, it is not rude, it does not seek its own interests, it is not quick-tempered, it does not brood over injury, it does not rejoice over wrongdoing but rejoices with the truth. It bears all things, believes all things, hopes all things, endures all things. . . .

At present we see indistinctly, as in a mirror, but then face to face. At present, I know partially; then I shall know fully, as I am fully known. So faith, hope, love remain, these three; but the greatest of these is love.

1 John 4:7-13
God's Love and Christian Life

Beloved, let us love one another, because love is of God; everyone who loves is begotten by God and knows God. Whoever is without love does not know God, for God is love. In this way the love of God was revealed to us: God sent his only Son into the world so that we might have life through him. In this is love: not that we have loved God, but that he loved us and sent his Son as expiation for our sins. Beloved, if God so loved us, we also must love one another. No one has ever seen God. Yet, if we love one another, God remains in us, and his love is brought to perfection in us. This is how we know that we remain in him and he in us, that he has given us of his Spirit.

Romans 8:35, 37-39
God's Indomitable Love in Christ

What will separate us from the love of Christ? Will anguish, or distress, or persecution, or famine, or nakedness, or peril, or the sword? . . .

No, in all these things we conquer overwhelmingly through him who loved us.

For I am convinced that neither death, nor life, not angels, nor principalities, nor present things, nor future things, nor powers, nor height, nor depth, nor any other creature will be able to separate us from the love of God in Christ Jesus our Lord.

Healing
and
Hope

Heal me, Lord, that I may be healed;
Save me, that I may be saved,
for it is you whom I praise.
　　　　　—Jeremiah 17:14

chapter seven

Healing and Hope

My dear friend,

In the scriptural part of this chapter we read some beautiful stories of Jesus healing people physically. Do I believe these stories? Yes I do. Given the nature of Jesus' earthly ministry, I do not have a lot of trouble believing that Jesus healed people from physical suffering.

As I look about me I notice that physical healings (cures) are rare. Does that mean that we are wasting our time praying for healing? Are we kidding ourselves to think we can be "cured" from AIDS? Absolutely not. God has told us to ask for whatever it is we need and I want more than anything for God to heal you and me from AIDS.

The main thing to remember is that healings do happen and are happening with people with all types of diseases. Healing takes place because the recipient believes it can happen. Thus, healing is not a spectator sport. No matter what type of healing takes place, physical or emotional, keep in mind that the person receiving the healing has an active faith and believes that healing is possible.

When it comes to healing and wanting to be physically healthy there is a difficult question that you and I must first answer. The question is, "Do we *want* to live?" Now I know at first, when told we are HIV positive or have ARC or AIDS, the natural response is, "Of course I want to live!" Life does not confront most people our age with this question.

Honestly, it takes a lot of courage and soul searching to ask yourself this question and be ready for an answer. I say all this because healing cannot take place until you know for sure that you *want* to live in this world the way it is now. There are no guarantees about how this world will continue to take shape. Are we ready for all that uncertainty?

To pray for healing implies that you and I are ready to do whatever it takes for us to do to live. There is no easy way out. To ask for healing, to work for healing and to hope for healing takes a lot of consistent work. If we want healing we need to know for what and/or for whom are we being healed? Why and for whom do we want to go on living? Are we asking for healing just because we fear death or are we getting a clearer focus on our purpose in life? Each of us has his or her own answer to this question; it is crucial that each of us knows what the answer is.

Not long ago there was a symposium in Los Angeles for long term survivors of AIDS. This was a gathering of women and men who had lived at least five years since receiving a diagnosis of AIDS. They drew up a list of characteristics that the long term survivors shared. Paramount on this list of common traits is that each one had had a renewal in his or her spiritual life. It didn't matter whether this renewal was in God, Jesus Christ, Yahweh, Buddha, or some other Higher Power known by other names. Each of these participants felt a contact through prayer and meditation with a reality higher than and outside of themselves. Here are women and men who have suffered over a period of five years still hoping and believing in healing. These men and women are living out a very important truth: *there is no such thing as false hope.*

Let me give you an example of what I am expressing to you. Recently I finished reading a Russian novel, *Children of the Arbat,* by Anatoli Rybakov. The protagonist, Sasha, is a young man falsely accused by the secret police of trying to subvert the government. The Russian government condemns Sasha to a camp of hard labor in Siberia for life. In an instant everything that was important to this young man was taken from him and replaced with darkness and suffering. Throughout his ordeal Sasha maintains a spirit that he will make the best of what is happening to him and that one day he would return home to his family. How does he do this in face of such overwhelming odds? Towards the end of the novel, the author writes of Sasha:

"Hope had preserved his humanity.
The goal had kept him alive."

Where I have experienced and witnessed the greatest amount of healing has been in my own emotional and spiritual life. With story after story people with AIDS or ARC tell me how they have experienced real healing from past emotional wounds. Through forgiving themselves and others, many of us with AIDS are learning how to live one day at a time with a certain amount of joy and hope. I am talking about real joy and real hope. Where there was darkness and panic before, I find people reconciled to God and to others. Each healing is unique. It is as if they and God found their way back to each other. I call that real healing.

No one, myself included, can sit here and promise you that either one of us will be physically healed from AIDS. You well know that if I did promise healing, I would be trying to sell you snake oil. Believe me, when first diagnosed with AIDS, I bought a lot of snake oil!

I can promise you this. If you work at it and get the right support and help, you can experience a real inner healing of your soul that radically changes the quality of your life for the better. Some would say it doesn't happen, but men and women with AIDS are feeling an inner sense of serenity in the midst of all this garish pain and suffering. The reason I boldly promise you this is that my own experience and the people I know who have AIDS constantly tell me that this deep inner healing is more common than you might at first believe.

Deep healing first takes place whenever we accept this sickness and learn to live with it. I didn't say, "like it," but *accept* that it is a part of my life today. I found that as I accepted AIDS I grew more peaceful and less anxious. Where once before I thought only darkness and pain awaited me, I now see that I have many new friends whom I love who are fighting AIDS with me.

Numerous research articles point to the conclusion that having and maintaining a positive and hopeful attitude has a direct, positive effect on peoples' immune systems. Not only do these people feel better living out their lives, but we are talking about positive physical results that take place with our bodies.

My friend, I mentioned that it takes a lot of work for healing to take place. There is a practical side to healing. You need to pay close attention to the attitudes of the people around you.

Let me give you an example. A specialist in a large AIDS clinic asked me to tell him the alternative treatments (vitamins and supplements) that I was taking. Then this doctor dismissed all my efforts by saying, "I will tell you what I tell all my patients, take that stuff if you like the taste of it better than peanut butter." This AIDS doctor was going by the A.M.A. book but in effect was removing all the hope I had for any type of recovery. I quit listening to him even though I liked him.

My friend, please do not dismiss lightly the positive results that hope can have in your life! You and I have to combat overwhelming public negative feelings about this disease. Most people, including your family and friends, only know this disease through the news media which paints a very bleak picture. I can recall the time a nurse in the hospital was chatting with me while giving me some medication. Without thinking, the nurse said to me, "Well you know, people with this disease never really get better." Protect yourself from comments that medical professionals, family and friends make that are negative and contain no hope.

Jeremiah 30:17, The Restoration

For I will restore you to health;
of your wounds I will heal
you, says the LORD.

Mark 5:
Jairus' Daughter and the Woman with a Hemorrhage

There was a woman afflicted with hemorrhages for twelve years. She had suffered greatly at the hands of many doctors and had spent all that she had. Yet she was not helped but only grew worse. She had heard about Jesus and came up behind him in the crowd and touched his cloak. She said, "If I touch his clothes, I shall be cured." Immediately her flow of blood dried up. She felt in her body that she was healed of her affliction. Jesus, aware at once that power had gone our from him, turned around in the crowd and asked, "Who has touched my clothes?" But his disciples said to him, "You see how the crowd is pressing upon you, and yet you ask, 'Who touched me?'" And he looked around to see who had done it. The woman, realizing what had happened to her, approached in fear and trembling. She fell down before Jesus and told him the whole truth. He said to her, "Daughter, your faith has saved you. Go in peace and be cured of your affliction."

Luke 4:40-41, Other Healings

At sunset, all who had people sick with various diseases brought them to him. He laid his hands on each of them and cured them. And demons also came out from many, shouting, "You are the Son of God." But he rebuked them and did not allow them to speak because they knew that he was the Messiah.

Luke 9:2, The Mission of the Twelve

. . . and he sent them to proclaim the kingdom of God and to heal the sick.

John 9:1-7, The Man Born Blind

As he passed by he saw a man blind from birth. His disciples asked him, "Rabbi, who sinned, this man or his parents, that he was born blind?"

Jesus answered, "Neither he nor his parents sinned; it is so that the works of God might be made visible through him. We have to do the works of the one who sent me while it is day. Night is coming when no one can work. While I am in the world, I am the light of the world."

When he said this, he spat on the ground and made clay with the saliva, and smeared the clay on his eyes, and said to him, "Go wash in the Pool of Siloam" (which means Sent). So he went and washed, and came back able to see.

*Comfort
and
Strength*

Blessed are they who mourn,
for they will be comforted.
—Matthew 5:4

chapter eight

Comfort and Strength

My dear friend,

I feel very close to you as I write this letter. One of my greatest sources of comfort and strength through this ordeal has been to get to know someone like you. Those of us who are suffering this disease find ourselves bonded together in a special way. I know I count on your being there when I need you and I want to be here for you.

A profound source of comfort and strength has been letting people love me. I am talking about taking in someone's free offer of love without figuring out how I was going to repay them and even the score. Letting people love me and receiving as gift all they do for me is my gift to them. Through this experience I have learned that people love me for who I am more than for what I can do. This experience, when felt and not just talked about, touches on the mystery of God.

All my life I have been a caregiver. With AIDS I have had to learn to let go of trying to take care of the world.

Instead, I have had to learn that taking care of *ourselves* is our number one priority. You and I have to do things for ourselves that we may not have the energy even to explain to others (and thereby continue to take care of them).

With AIDS there is physical suffering and enormous amounts of uncertainty. I want to speak a little about another source of suffering. I am referring to those dark inner voices that wear us down and tell us that our life is hopeless. This is the worst type of suffering as it usually erodes all hope.

I have noticed that these dark inner voices start the minute I feel a fever coming on or fatigue setting in. Whenever I put too much trust in statistics you can bet I am setting myself up for a downfall. An example of this is waiting for a blood report to come back and tell me that I am feeling okay and that I am getting better. I can be feeling fine, but when I hear that my white blood cell count is way down I immediately start feeling sick and hopeless. Whenever this happens I start imagining the worst.

Remember when you first met someone and you'd either ask or guess their astrological sign? Maybe you wanted to know where they came out on the Myers-Briggs scale or even their number on the Sufi Enneagram. We have replaced all that with wanting to know a person's T-Cell count, P24 antigen count, or even white and red blood cell count.

Now we want to know the medical "statistics" about ourselves and others. Keep this in mind: Statistics, blood counts, and results from tests do not consider your will to live and ability to fight back. I have yet to read one medical report that included measurements of faith and hope. Statistical reports leave one important feature out of their reports: YOU.

I remember reading a statistic that said that the median time of survival for PWA's (persons with AIDS) is 18 months from date of diagnosis. This month I reach the "magic" 18 months. Some weeks ago I started feeling panic and a lot of fear of death because, according to statistics, I will die soon. You and I have to watch out for all kinds of emotional viruses that can hurt us as much as the physical ones. Do not listen to anyone or any article which presumes to play God by telling you how much time you have left. Your life and your death belong to you and God alone. You have much more power in this area than you might at first believe.

A Synergistic Approach

I bet that since receiving your diagnosis of being HIV positive several new words sprinkle your daily vocabulary. "Synergistic" is one of these new words we've all come to know and love. Synergistic means "working together." When one drug increases the effectiveness of another one, it works synergistically with that drug. Sometimes taking two or three drugs is more powerful than if you just took one of the drugs alone.

Comfort and strength come from three powerful spiritual drugs: Faith, Hope and Love. My experience is that when combined with each other they work synergistically and produce greater results. I hope by now you have had some moving experience that renewed your belief in faith, hope and love. Experiencing these three spiritual realities can produce a deep feeling of well being and purpose in life, feelings of comfort and strength.

Here is the catch. When you need comfort and strength you want to feel hopeful about the future. It is always a tricky business trying to conjure up feelings—it usually does not work.

The temptation here is if you cannot produce these good feelings by sheer force of your will, you may soon believe they don't exist. We judge the value of our prayer by whether or not we get the desired feeling. At this point the dark voices turn up their volume and try to lure us into deeper despair. I've already mentioned how you have to protect yourself from those around you. You also have to protect yourself from your dark self.

I have found myself saying things like, "Look at all I do to fight back and nothing works!" "God doesn't love me!" "Why not just give in, I'm tired of fighting a battle I cannot win." I notice healthy people running around laughing and smiling, and I react by concentrating on what I don't have and forgetting what I do have. At times like these I feel like a loser and a victim.

My friend, I can no more remove these ugly feelings when they come over me than I can produce good feelings at will. I have found that the ugly feelings, when left alone and allowed to pass through me (not repressed), sooner or later do go away. It is as if we don't have ugly and angry feelings, *they have us!* I have experienced comfort and strength when I took the courage to feel my darkest moments with someone who just listened and did not try to take them away. Usually this would entail my listener feeling the darkness with me and not offering a facile solution.

This dryness of spiritual feeling is natural to the human race. We all go through a few peak experiences followed by many valleys of darkness or mundane routine. It is during the day to day routine that we have the greatest chance to advance in the spiritual life. During peak experiences we promise God anything because we feel so good. It is as if God then leaves us alone so that we can put into practice (faith, hope and love) that which we believe in.

Faith uttered but never lived out is dead faith. Hope felt in deep prayer but forgotten in pain is useless. Love, so much talked about, remains unreal unless we pay its price in action.

Isaiah 35:3-7
Israel's Deliverance

Strengthen the hands that are feeble,
make firm the knees that are
weak,
Say to those whose hearts are
frightened:
Be strong, fear not!
Here is your God,
he comes with vindication;
With divine recompense
he comes to save you.
Then will the eyes of the blind
be opened,
the ears of the deaf be cleared;
Then will the lame leap like a
stag,
then the tongue of the dumb
will sing.

Streams will burst forth in the
desert, and rivers in the steppe.
The burning sands will become
pools,
and the thirsty ground,
springs of water;
The abode where jackals lurk
will be a marsh for the reed
and papyrus.

Matthew 5:1-12
The Sermon on the Mount

When he saw the crowds, he went up the mountain, and after he had sat down, his disciples came to him. He began to teach them, saying:

The Beatitudes

"Blessed are the poor in spirit, for theirs is the kingdom of heaven. Blessed are they who mourn, for they will be comforted. Blessed are the meek, for they will inherit the land. Blessed are they who hunger and thirst for righteousness, for they will be satisfied. Blessed are the merciful, for they will be shown mercy. Blessed are the clean of heart, for they will see God. Blessed are the peacemakers, for they will be called children of God. Blessed are they who are persecuted for the sake of righteousness, for theirs is the kingdom of heaven.

Blessed are you when they insult you and persecute you and utter every kind of evil against you falsely because of me. Rejoice and be glad, for your reward will be great in heaven. Thus they persecuted the prophets who were before you."

Matthew 6:25-34
Dependence on God

"Therefore I tell you, do not worry about your life, what you will eat or drink or use for clothing. Look at the birds in the sky; they do not sow or reap, they gather nothing into barns, yet your heavenly Father feeds them. Are not you more important than they? Can any of you by worrying add a single moment to your life-span? Why are you anxious about clothes? Learn from the way the wild flowers grow. They do not work or spin. But I tell you that not even Solomon in all his splendor was clothed like one of them. If God so clothes the grass of the field, which grows today and is thrown into the oven tomorrow, will he not much more provide for you, O you of little faith? So do not worry and say, 'What are we to eat?' or 'What are we to drink?' or 'What are we to wear?' All these things the pagans seek. Your heavenly Father knows that you need them all. But seek first the kingdom of God and his righteousness, and all these things will be given you besides. Do not worry about tomorrow; tomorrow will take care of itself. Sufficient for a day is its own evil."

Death

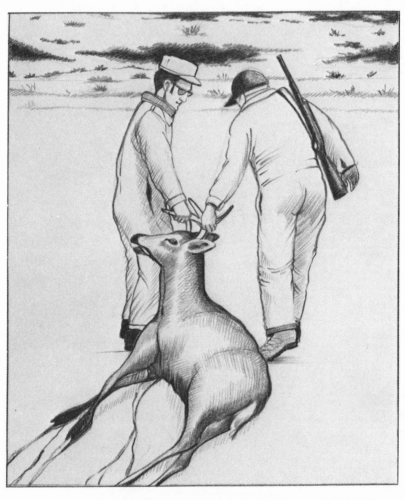

Father, into your hands
I commend my spirit.
   —Luke 23:46

chapter nine

Death

My dear friend,

I want to write this chapter and also I don't want to write it. I am afraid of death and it seems like such a sad and ugly subject that I want to omit it from this book. However, there are moments when you and I need to share our feelings about death. I want to be with you if this is one of those times for you. I won't leave you, nor will I try to change the subject.

Our culture goes out of its way to hide aging, physical weakness, and death itself. If we are not part of the youthful, Cola-generation, we are nobody. What is the second most asked question after "What is your name?" It's "What do you do?" Not, "Who are you?" or "Are you happy?," but "What do you do?"

In our culture if you are not doing anything or producing anything you might as well be dead. Rare is the moment that you will find an open and healthy discussion on death and dying. But you and I don't have the luxury of hiding and running from things. The song, "Some things are better left unsaid" (by Hall and Oates), may not be the best route for us to take.

There is another dilemma in writing to you on death. From the moment that I knew I had lymphoma and AIDS I subscribed to what I call the "maintain a positive and hopeful attitude" school of thought. You hear a lot of different things from New Age Spirituality. Most of it is very useful and good. What I have in mind here is especially Louise Hay and Dr. Bernie Segal. Their insights into the disease process and the positive part we can play in the process are invaluable.

I believe in and regularly use meditation tapes that reduce stress and emphasize hope and positive healing. I have believed in a positive attitude long before AIDS. On my ordination card in 1978, I placed a saying from Saint Thérèse of Lisieux, France:

"We can never have too much hope in God."

So as I started to battle a deadly lymphoma, I had a lot of hope that I could beat the cancer. I also have hope that soon there will be a safe medical way to fight the AIDS virus. My belief then and now is: There is never anything called false hope. Hope is real, hope is powerful, hope is holy.

The dilemma in which some of us find ourselves is this: if we talk at all about death, does that mean we are "giving up"? At the same time, if we *don't* talk about death as a possibility, are we in some acute state of denial? This has implications in our daily lives: Do we try to live and plan our lives, or do we prepare to die and try to come to some acceptance and peace about our predicament? This alone has caused me a lot of tension and anxiety.

It is important to talk about death. Since you and I have known that we are seropositive to the AIDS virus, we have thought a lot about death and dying. Remember the panic that the very thought of having AIDS and dying brought over you? Remember when you first told friends or family members what was going on? Recall their initial reactions? Some who had never faced death would say to you, "Well, you know, we all have to die someday also." Some friends would tell me that they could be hit by a truck and die that afternoon. What about the death you felt when a close friend would inform you, "I've let go of you" (meaning: "you can die now"). Here I am trying to stay attached to life and a friend tells me he is letting me go!

Not long ago I had to drop out of a doctorate program in clinical psychology because of this illness. Having spent over four years on this degree, I needed only to write my dissertation. I felt a real death in letting go of my degree. It hurt and I hated it; I mourned not being able to finish my goal. I remember telling a friend that this was a real death to me. I felt that if I died of AIDS the physical death would be the easiest part of the whole process.

It is these little and big deaths we suffer along the way that can be so difficult and devastating to us. There is a lot of death and dying that takes place in our relationships with our family and friends. Sickness changes everything! Some, if not most, people close to us (family or friends) can only go so far with us as we journey with this disease. I, like you, have had good friends go months before they would call or want to see me. How do you play "catch up" after all you've been through in *two weeks*, let alone *months*? There is a real death that happens to the relationship at that time.

So many of our brothers and sisters with AIDS find themselves forced to move from their homes, to lose their jobs and become totally reliant on strangers for help. You and I have had to let go of things we used to do physically or mentally. To me these are all the little and big deaths we undergo. I fear that death will take me by surprise. Undergoing all these other deaths, we know what death is and that it doesn't have to be this big unknown scary event. You and I already know how to die. We've done it too many times.

I don't have easy solutions in understanding the mystery of death. I do believe that, like birth, death is a deep mystery. Each death is personal and unique because it belongs to the individual. If you are close to death I pray that you make the event yours and not necessarily what those around you want it to be. If you want to fight up to your last breath, please, I hope that you do! Do it your way! I believe that death is not a sign of failure nor is it the end.

We can only approach understanding the great mysteries in life through our imagination. Several times

I have dialogued with death. I did this using a journal-ing technique called "Active Imagination." I wrote out my voice in my journal and asked death to speak to me. You may or may not want to do this type of activity. Each time I did this dialogue with death, I gained a lot of peace and insight for myself. Death told me several times that he was my brother and that he comes from God. Death also told me that he was holy and his only purpose in life was to do the will of God. Another time death told me that God had ordained that death be the door, the threshold through which each soul passes to eternal life. You find out in your death what you would not believe in your life: you are love. . . .

Psalm 23: The Lord, Shepherd and Host

The LORD is my shepherd; I
shall not want.

In verdant pastures he gives
me repose;
Beside restful waters he leads
me;
he refreshes my soul.
He guides me in right paths
for his name's sake.
Even though I walk in the dark
valley
I fear no evil; for you are at
my side
With your rod and your staff
that give me courage.

You spread the table before
me
in the sight of my foes;
You anoint my head with oil;
my cup overflows.
Only goodness and kindness
follow me
all the days of my life;
And I shall dwell in the house
of the LORD
for years to come.

Wisdom 4:7-8, On Early Death

But the just man, though he die
early, shall be at rest.
For the age that is honorable
comes not with the passing
of time,
nor can it be measured in
terms of years.

Luke 22:41-44, The Agony in the Garden

After withdrawing about a stone's throw from them and kneeling, Jesus prayed, saying, "Father, if you are willing, take this cup away from me; still, not my will but yours be done." And to strengthen him an angel from heaven appeared to him. He was in such agony and he prayed so fervently that his sweat became like drops of blood falling on the ground.

Luke 23:33-35 The Crucifixion

When they came to the place called the Skull, they crucified him and the criminals there, one on his right, the other on his left. Then Jesus said, "Father, forgive them, they know not what they do." They divided his garments by casting lots. The people stood by and watched; the rulers, meanwhile, sneered at him and said, "He saved others, let him save himself if he is the chosen one, the Messiah of God."

John 14:1-3, Last Supper Discourses

"Do not let your hearts be troubled. You have faith in God; have faith also in me. In my Father's house there are many dwelling places. If there were not, would I have told you that I am going to prepare a place for you? And if I go and prepare a place for you, I will come back again and take you to myself, so that where I am you also may be."

Acts 7:55-60, Stephen's Martyrdom

But he [Stephen], filled with the holy Spirit, looked up intently to heaven and saw the glory of God and Jesus standing at the right hand of God, and he said, "Behold, I see the heavens opened and the Son of Man standing at the right hand of God." But they cried out in a loud voice, covered their ears, and rushed upon him together. They threw him out of the city, and began to stone him. The witnesses laid down their cloaks at the feet of a young man named Saul. As they were stoning Stephen, he called out, "Lord Jesus, receive my spirit." Then he fell to his knees and cried out in a loud voice, "Lord, do not hold this sin against them"; and when he said this, he fell asleep.

Resurrection

Behold, I make all things new.
—Revelations 21:5

chapter ten

Resurrection

My dear friend,

As I write you this letter it happens to be Spring and the Easter season! I live in the Midwest where we eagerly await Spring.

The other day I looked out at the frozen land and saw nothing but bleak, gray sky, and barren trees, and I felt such a cold chill running up and down my spine. Everything looked so dead.

Then what happens? I turn around and look out at the very same scene. Now tulips, daffodils, and fragrant hyacinths are getting ready to bloom. The trees I observe now are all budded with that airy light spring-green touch and I feel new life surging within me. The people I know seem to feel better and I observe more smiles than I do in winter. Something is happening quietly right before our eyes. What is it?

As a priest I have always felt that during these holy feasts (Christmas and Easter) I should have the "perfect" thing to say to explain these mysteries. The spiritual aspect of Christmas has always been so much easier for me to understand. Four weeks before Christmas, during Advent, we have the image of waiting for a promise to come to fruition. The promise is new life—a child. I do not have children like you may have, but having brothers and sisters, nieces and nephews, I can appreciate it. Birth is something we experience daily; we know it happens and can touch it.

I don't know about you, but I love kids. I love the challenge to win them over and communicate with them on whatever level they are on. Whenever I am in public and I encounter a small child I try to make some contact with the child. This contact can be a smile, a funny face or just talking with them as we find ourselves in the same checkout line. Especially if the child talks to me first I always try to answer them back and play with them. I used to be so afraid of doing this in public with children because of how it might appear to their parents. I am no longer afraid of making contact with children in public and, clearly, it's an enjoyable experience for both of us. Children are real, right in front of you and you just see so much life and potential smiling at you with big darting eyes. Other than the commercialization which I abhor, I think I understand Christmas.

What about Easter and Resurrection? I can give you a dogmatic explanation of what believers put their faith in when it comes to explaining or defining Easter and the Resurrection. I would write you one in this epistle if I thought for one second that it would clear up the matter. But the truth is that I have difficulty relating to what all happened so many years ago to Jesus; an event we call the Resurrection. I know that Jesus was born and that that was Christmas. Okay, I was born and I have been experiencing life ever since.

But the Resurrection has happened only once, and only to Jesus. The rest of us are waiting for the Second Coming of Christ and can only imagine what Resurrection is and what it is like. To complicate matters, there are all those other stories clustered around the crucifixion: Jesus being executed, taken down from the cross and buried. Now, while I get a warm glow, with tender feelings when I think about the Christmas story, I feel scared and in the dark when I recall the stories surrounding the passion and resurrection of Christ.

Yet it is the Resurrection upon which we base our entire faith in Life itself. For many years I have puzzled over how to understand and actively live the Resurrection. This Easter I got an insight that I want to share with you and see if it helps you as much as it did me. Let me first recall one of the many stories in the New Testament about those first few hours and days after the Resurrection. This comes from John 20:11-19, and involves Jesus after his Resurrection with his devoted friend Mary Magdalene.

An Easter Story

Mary stayed outside the tomb weeping. And as she wept, she bent over into the tomb and saw two angels in white sitting there, one at the head and one at the feet where the body of Jesus had been. And they said to her, "Woman, why are you weeping?" She said to them, "They have taken my Lord, and I don't know where they laid him."

When she had said this, she turned around and saw Jesus there, but did not know it was Jesus. Jesus said to her, "Woman, why are you weeping? Whom are you looking for?" She thought it was the gardener and said to him, "Sir, if you carried him away, tell me where you laid him, and I will take him."

Jesus said to her, "Mary." She turned and said to him in Hebrew, "Rabbouni," which means Teacher. Jesus said to her, "Stop holding on to me, for I have not yet ascended to the Father. But go to my brothers and tell them, 'I am going to my Father and your Father, to my God and your God.'"

Mary of Magdala went and announced to the disciples, "I have seen the Lord!" and what he had told her.

Keep in mind a few important facts. We know that before she encountered Jesus, Mary Magdalene was a prostitute and thus had developed a sharp street sense about her. As such, Mary Magdalene could size men up quickly and figure out what all was going on at any certain moment. Upon meeting Jesus and feeling his love and acceptance Mary Magdalene became one of his disciples. Out of love for Jesus she followed him from town to town. Mary Magdalene knew what Jesus looked like, what his tone of voice sounded like and when he was present to anyone.

Here in this scripture passage we have Mary Magdalene going out on Easter morning to the tomb where she had seen them place the crucified and dead Jesus. Immediately she encounters the Resurrection as she finds herself looking right into the eyes of Jesus. Mary Magdalene is staring at the Resurrection and she mistakes Jesus (the Resurrection) for something as common and ordinary as a gardener. Mary encounters this deep mystery and she sees nothing but common ordinary life. It is not until Jesus speaks her name that the reality of what and who she sees hits her and she says to him, "Rabbouni!" a sign of deep respect and recognition.

The Resurrection is like this—right before our eyes, we see it every day. Because the Resurrection and the promise of New Life surrounds us here and now, more often than not we miss it. Resurrection is not necessarily something we are awaiting that is so totally new and foreign to us. Resurrection is happening now.

I believe in the Resurrection on the Last Day and in Life Eternal. This deep mystery is all around us and I see it especially in Spring. I also see it when two people forgive each other and the relationship that was dead comes alive. I see Resurrection when I see people caring for each other and when someone helps another feel good about herself or himself. I feel Resurrection every time I am real sick and instead of dying I get better and live. Dear friend, these examples I have given you are but images of what The Resurrection will be like, but the very idea of it excites me. Believe in your unique images of the Resurrection!

Since I am alone with you I want to let you know something that I believe in my heart and soul. In The Resurrection there will be no more oppression nor injustice. In the next Life there will be no more lies, no deceit. God will transform all your tears, pain and suffering to the beautiful person you are becoming right now! Life is right before us. We touch the extraordinary and mistake it for the ordinary. You are beautiful and I love you!

John 11:17-27, 33-44
The Raising of Lazarus

When Jesus arrived, he found that Lazarus had already been in the tomb for four days. Now Bethany was near Jersualem, only about two miles away. And many of the Jews had come to Martha and Mary to comfort them about their brother. When Martha heard that Jesus was coming, she went to meet him; but Mary sat at home. Martha said to Jesus, "Lord, if you had been here, my brother would not have died. [But] even now I know that whatever you ask God, God will give you." Jesus said to her, "Your brother will rise." Martha said to him, "I know he will rise, in the resurrection on the last day." Jesus told her, "I am the resurrection and the life; whoever believes in me, even if he dies, will live, and everyone who lives and believes in me will never die. Do you believe this?" She said to him, "Yes, Lord. I have come to believe that you are the Messiah, the Son of God, the one who is coming into the world."

When Jesus saw her weeping and the Jews who had come with her weeping, he became perturbed and deeply troubled, and said, "Where have you laid him?" They said to him, "Sir, come and see." And Jesus wept. So the Jews said, "See how he loved him." But some of them said, "Could not the one who opened the eyes of the blind man have done something so that this man would not have died?"

So Jesus, perturbed again, came to the tomb. It was a cave and a stone lay across it. Jesus said, "Take away the stone." Martha, the dead man's sister, said to him,

"Lord, by now there will be a stench; he has been dead for four days." Jesus said to her, "Did I not tell you that if you believe you will see the glory of God?" So they took away the stone. And Jesus raised his eyes and said, "Father, I thank you for hearing me. I know that you always hear me; but because of the crowd here I have said this, that they may believe that you sent me."

And when he had said this, he cried out in a loud voice, "Lazarus, come out!" The dead man came out, tied hand and foot with burial bands, and his face was wrapped in a cloth. So Jesus said to them, "Untie him and let him go."

John 20:1-9
The Empty Tomb

On the first day of the week, Mary of Magdala came to the tomb early in the morning, while it was still dark, and saw the stone removed from the tomb. So she ran and went to Simon Peter and to the other disciple whom Jesus loved, and told them, "They have taken the Lord from the tomb, and we don't know where they put him." So Peter and the other disciple went out and came to the tomb. They both ran, but the other disciple ran faster than Peter and arrived at the tomb first; he bent down and saw the burial cloths there, but did not go in. When Simon Peter arrived after him, he went into the tomb and saw the burial cloths there, and the cloth that had covered his head, not with the burial cloths but rolled up in a separate place. Then the other disciple also went in, the one who had arrived at the tomb first, and he saw and believed. For they did not yet understand the scripture that he had to rise from the dead.

Revelation 21:1-7
The New Heaven and the New Earth

Then I saw a new heaven and a new earth. The former heaven and the former earth had passed away, and the sea was no more. I also saw the holy city, a new Jerusalem, coming down out of heaven from God, prepared as a bride adorned for her husband. I heard a loud voice from the throne saying, "Behold, God's dwelling is with the human race. He will dwell with them and they will be his people and God himself will always be with them as their God. He will wipe away every tear from their eyes, and there shall be no more death or mourning, wailing or pain, for the old order has passed away."

The one who sat on the throne said, "Behold, I make all things new." Then he said, "Write these words down, for they are trustworthy and true." He said to me, "They are accomplished. I am the Alpha and the Omega, the beginning and the end. To the thirsty I will give a gift from the spring of life-giving water. The victor will inherit these gifts, and I shall be his God, and he will be my son."

Prayer
and
Adoration

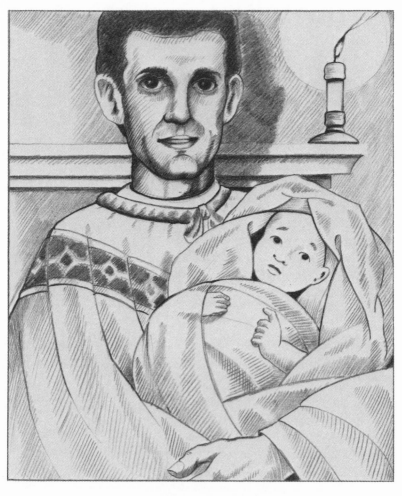

Be still and know that
I am God.
                                    —Psalm 46:11

chapter eleven

Prayer and Adoration

My dear friend,

I feel sad as I write you. This epistle on prayer and adoration will be the last one that I write you for awhile. It may be that I can write more letters at some later time, but that is out of my hands. All I know is how much I have loved our times together and how I care for you. Suffering has such a potential to bring us close together. Suffering can cut through darkness and the superficial so fast. Through suffering you and I are learning what the essentials are in life: faith, hope and love.

Honoring Life

I may have mentioned to you before how I believe that we pray much more than we realize. We pray in our pain, tears and joys. Our very being is a living prayer reaching out to God in thanksgiving for life itself. Prayer is who we are, not just what we do. There are many times when I have felt down and out and I wondered, Why do I even fight this disease?, Why do I

111

go through all this pain? You know by now that I have no easy answers to these questions. What I want you to know is that I get some comfort in those dark moments when my prayer tells me that I am trying to honor Life.

To honor Life—it seems too simple to be helpful. Consider this line from Psalm 12:4-5. I read it one day when I was in the pits. Horrible fatigue had a grip on me that day, not to mention diarrhea and a hot fever. Here is the psalm I prayed:

"Give light to my eyes, Lord, lest I sleep in death, and my enemy say: 'I have overcome him.' " All my dark, inner voices started barking and tearing at me like mad dogs. I thought that with all I have gone through I could not take anymore suffering. Had I not done my share of suffering? Yet here I was getting another diagnosis. Why so much and why me? At this time my enemy said to me, "Where is your God now? How come your health only gets worse and more painful while you do all that praying?" I can take just so much suffering and after that cut-off point I lose hope and no longer believe in God. My friend, as we both know this is a very dark place to be. In these moments how can I maintain with you that there is no such thing as false hope?

Hope, prayer and honoring Life all seem to me to be different aspects of the same mystery that we are living. When I say that there is no false hope, I am not saying there is no such thing as pain. Therein lies a lot of confusion. I can have hope that the pain will go away and never come back. Life does not always work that way.

No matter how much pain we are in at present, it is always possible that there can be more pain ahead. Hope does its greatest healing when we are in our darkest moments.

Prayer and Adoration

There are many types of prayer. There are formal prayers that we utter either alone or with others. Religious ceremonies with their prescribed set of prayers are vital to our spiritual growth. This type of praying can help us to feel like a part of a community.

Some people get hung up if they don't pray "official" prayers. So many times we may want to pray but become too tired or sick to recite our prayers. When we are sick, our desire to pray and to communicate with God is itself the best prayer we can have at that time. What is required of us in all of this is trust and faith in our total and complete acceptance in God. Our prayer deepens as we believe more and more in the fact that God accepts and loves us. Prayer is so much more than just "saying our prayers." It is God giving God's very life to us and our receiving this gift.

Adoration is not a modern, "in" word and could turn some people off. But I think it is a beautiful word that accurately describes an aspect and deep-seated need we all have even if we would rather call it something else. Adoration is prayer, a unique experience in prayer. I think what makes adoration different from other types of prayer is that adoration *happens to us* instead of it being anything we can control or do.

Most of the time when we are going to meditate or pray we are in control. We pick out the scripture, topic, or meditation tape with which we would like to pray. We choose the loved ones for whom we want to pray and usually we have selected the place and time of day for our prayer. We personalize and individualize our prayer to a great extent.

Adoration is prayer, a unique type of personal prayer. Its uniqueness is that it happens to us, it takes over in small ways and sometimes big ways. Adoration of God can take place when you least expect it and in places you may not have chosen to pray. Let me try to explain and please bear with me.

My friend, please keep in mind that I am only sharing my experiences with you. You may or may not have experienced what I am describing to you. Be at peace! I mention all of this because I think many people do experience something like adoration but may not know exactly what is going on. You may be closer to God than you realize. In fact, I know you are.

With authentic adoration of God, an experience of God takes place. To talk to God is one thing and a very good thing indeed. We talk to God all the time and this makes up the majority of our time with God. This is all well and good. *To experience God*, the unknown, the unseen and the unheard of is the result of some type of direct action from God. You can be anywhere at anytime and suddenly you realize that there is an unseen presence that lives its own life and in whose presence you shudder. From one second to the next you know something is very different, and you know you did not cause it. Nor can you control it.

This direct experience of God comes about in the silence of the heart, in the quiet of the soul, in the solitude of an encounter with that which cannot be seen nor truly explained. It brings with it a deep inner peace that money cannot buy. *In this special moment it is God reaching out for you.* God is praying through you and you alone in a second or in an hour—time and space are irrelevant. During this time it matters naught what is your religious background or the name you use to address God.

I know when these moments come on because life as we know it, with normal thoughts and feelings, seems to suspend. You feel a special presence over which you do not have control. Like an automatic reflex, it does not matter what I was thinking or feeling before it comes on, I find myself telling God how much I love God. I could have been in great physical pain and emotional confusion seconds before and suddenly words spring from my heart of great tenderness with very little effort on my part.

It is like a well from which spring water comes pouring out with no effort on my part. Instead of asking for something or asking some great question about life, all I can do is try to reassure God of my fathomless love for

God. It seems that when this happens the feeling will go on forever. In a moment of time you see and hear eternity. I can only describe eternity at that moment as LOVE. People tell me that during this type of prayer they sometimes feel elated and so energized that they want to go paint the house, turn cartwheels in the front yard, or do anything to help them bear this burst of life-giving force that seems to have taken them over.

My experience of this type of prayer seems to happen in a flash. In a second or two everything stops and I see Life clearly. What makes it even more intense is that during this experience God shows me to myself with all my contradictions, weakness and ability to forget all that I am learning. But instead of making me feel bad about myself in those moments, it only makes me love God and God's creation more. No matter how close I feel to God in what seems to be a split second and forever at the same time, God is God and I am naturally, beautifully and in utter weakness, a small reflection of God.

My dear friend, this is why I believe that we become our prayer. I am and I love to be human in those moments. In those moments it seems that I can understand most of the sides to my personality. It is as if I am good, bad, living, dying, giving and taking all at the same time. I love my darkness as much as I love my brightness—for in the charity of God it is all accepted. In these moments of adoring God I know that I walk the earth with clay feet. The earth is where I belong with my human condition—a natural condition for me through which I attract God's attention.

The Prayer of Quiet

Let me try to summarize what I am sharing with you in regard to prayer and adoration. What I call "The Prayer of Quiet" is itself a dynamic example of adoration.

Sooner or later the prayer of quiet will come to you. Trust in it. It is a state of being with God that God deeply desires for you. God alone can bring about the prayer of quiet within you. In the prayer of quiet you do not fret "Am I praying?," "How am I doing?," "Have I prayed enough?" All these and other questions vanish from consciousness like an early morning fog at the rising of the sun.

With the prayer of quiet you forget about yourself and your performance (as if performances could get you closer to God!). You do not think or do, *you just are* with God and God is with you. Two hearts quietly beating, merging and remaining separate. There are times when the prayer of quiet is intense, but you only know this later upon reflection. In losing yourself in the prayer of quiet you become everything around you: the crisp morning air, the rising sun, the cool wet grass, the darkness of the night and the noises you hear all around you. All of these things lead and invite you to go beyond all that you see, touch and smell and to enter into the silence.

Go beyond whatever fear and panic threatens your deep inner peace. In this special silence of your heart there is no need to ask anything. You already "know."

This experience is a natural birthright of yours. Just as a child is born with this or that trait of his or her parents, so too have you inherited a spiritual trait from our loving creator to be able to rest deeply in the prayer of quiet. In this prayer of quiet you accomplish small things: Hope is renewed; courage is restored, real joy about Life is felt without a need to possess Life. In this prayer you sense a willingness to let Life pass through you so that you can move on. You "know" that in moving on you will live forever. It's very natural for you to be in the prayer of quiet.

You can go there.

You will go there.

You've already been there.

My friend, I love you and I miss you already.

Psalm 131: Humble Trust in God

O LORD, my heart is not proud,
nor are my eyes haughty;
I busy not myself with great
things,
nor with things too sublime
for me.
Nay rather, I have stilled and
quieted
my soul like a weaned child.
Like a weaned child on its
mother's lap,
so is my soul within me.
O Israel, hope in the LORD,
both now and forever.

Isaiah 6:1-8
Call of Isaiah

In the year King Uzziah died, I saw the LORD seated on a high and lofty throne, with the train of his garment filling the temple. Seraphim were stationed above; each of them had six wings: with two they veiled their feet, and with two they hovered aloft.

Holy, holy, holy is the LORD of hosts!" they cried one to the other. "All the earth is filled with his glory!" At the sound of that cry, the frame of the door shook and the house was filled with smoke.

Then I said, "Woe is me, I am doomed! For I am a man of unclean lips, living among a people of unclean lips; yet my eyes have seen the King, the LORD of hosts!" Then one of the seraphim flew to me, holding an ember which he had taken with tongs from the altar.

He touched my mouth with it. "See," he said, "now that this has touched your lips, your wickedness is removed, your sin purged."

Then I heard the voice of the LORD saying, "Whom shall I send? Who will go for us?" "Here I am," I said; "Send me!"

Colossians 1:13-20

He delivered us from the power of darkness and transferred us to the kingdom of his beloved Son, in whom we have redemption, the forgiveness of sins.

He is the image of the invisible
God,
the firstborn of all creation.
For in him were created all
things in heaven and on
earth,
the visible and the invisible,
whether thrones or dominions
or principalities or powers;
all things were created through
him and for him.
He is before all things,
and in him all things hold
together.
He is the head of the body, the
church.
He is the beginning, the
first-born from the dead,
that in all things he himself
might be preeminent.
For in him all the fullness was
pleased to dwell,
and through him to reconcile
all things for him,
making peace by the blood of
his cross
through him, whether those
on earth or those in heaven.

Notes on the Drawings

chapter one:　　The hart or dear or stag is an ancient symbol of the soul in search of God. The hart stands attentive and waiting.

chapter two:　　A young man plunged into darkness, with the eyes of the hart—bereft of comfort.

chapter three:　　Drawing after Caravaggio's dramatic rendering of "The Sacrifice of Isaac." Oppression is forced here; the child's grief and shock cry out as violence is about to take place . . . part of the horror is that the perpetrator is also the father.

chapter four:　　The lost soul entangled in a scene of briars or an underworld. Sin brings disorientation as well as suffering.

chapter five:　　The hands of one person caress the hand of another; an unspoken, gentle reconciliation is happening.

chapter six:　　The embrace and love of mother and child.

chapter seven:　　A woman shown recovering. Wounded by the IV which is also bringing healing, her thoughts are turning towards hope.

chapter eight:	Water is comfort and strength; a young man brings a young woman to the water; they bring each other comfort and strength.
chapter nine:	The dead deer or hart is carried off by the hunters. The continued image of the stag is now sacrificial, a "Christ-like" animal.
chapter ten:	Drawing after N.C. Wyeth's painting of a dear in *The Yearling*. The hart vibrant and alive almost dances with new life . . . . the risen One comes forth.
chapter eleven:	Holding and protecting the child, both the real child and the child within, can be prayer and adoration.